sun kissed
PUBLICATIONS, LLC

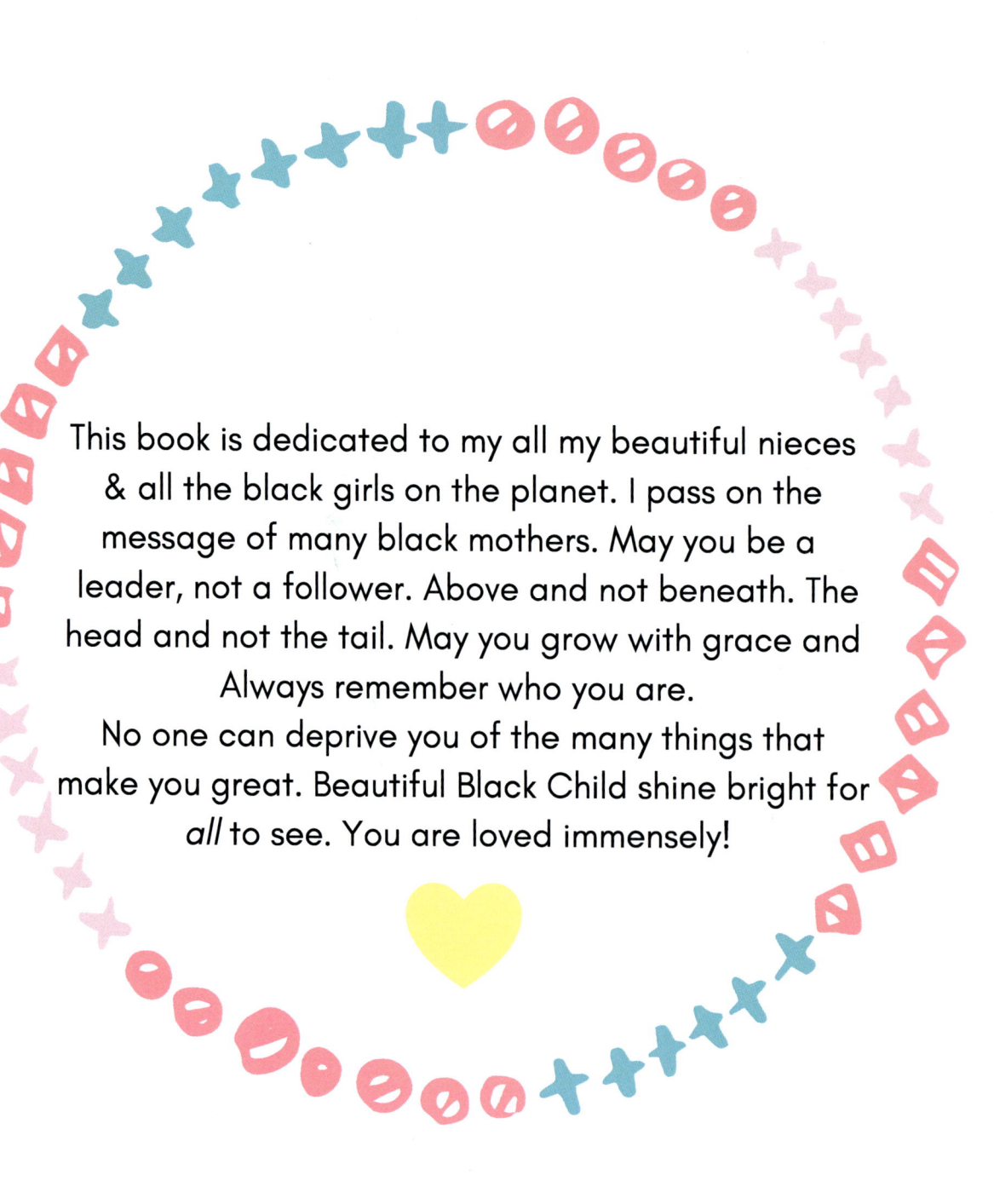

This book is dedicated to my all my beautiful nieces & all the black girls on the planet. I pass on the message of many black mothers. May you be a leader, not a follower. Above and not beneath. The head and not the tail. May you grow with grace and Always remember who you are.
No one can deprive you of the many things that make you great. Beautiful Black Child shine bright for *all* to see. You are loved immensely!

A

Animated

Black girl you are animated.

B

Blessed

Black girl you are blessed.

C

Confident

Black Girl YOU are confident!

D

Dominate

Black girl, you can dominate any stage or field.

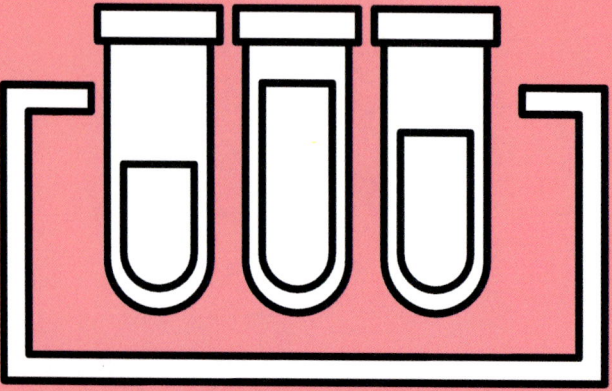

E

Excel

Black girl, you excel!

★★★★★

F

Fly

Black girl, you are FLY!

G
Graceful

Black girl, you are graceful, giving, and gorgeous.

H

Hopeful

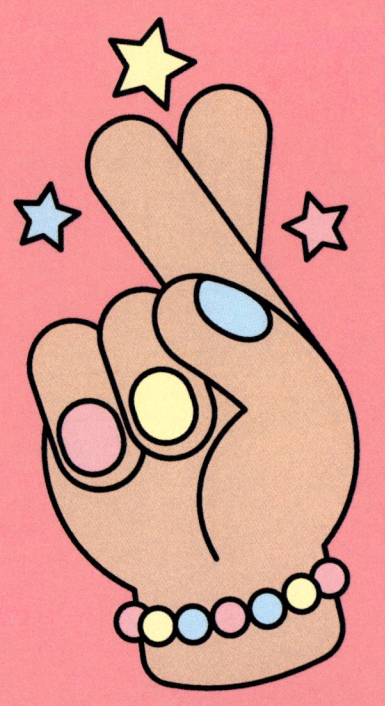

Black girl, you are happy & hopeful!

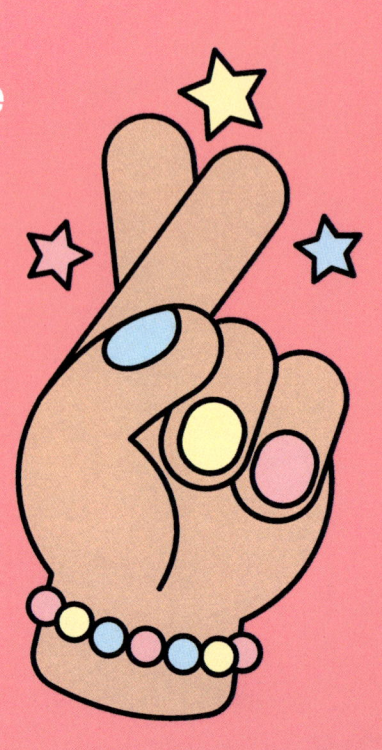

I

Intuitive

**Black girl, you are in-too-it-iv.
That means you can see beyond
what's in front of you.**

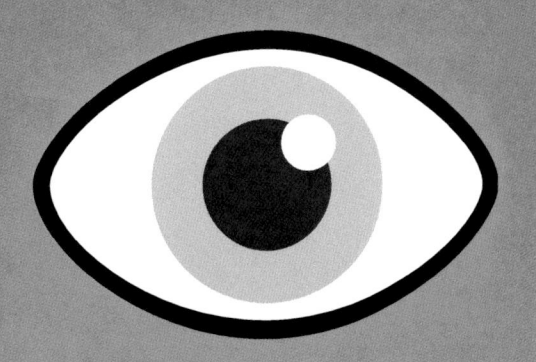

J

Joy

Black girl, your joy is your strength !

K

Kindness

Black girl, you win with Kindness.

L

Love

Black girl, you operate in love.

M

Magical

Black girl, you are simply magical!

N

Name

Black girl, your name is your identity. It is unique & beautiful! You're allowed to correct anyone who messes it up.

HELLO
my name is
Zyaire

O
Open

Black girl, you are not afraid to open your mouth and be heard!

OKAY!

P

Priceless

Black girl, you better know, you are PRICELESS. There is no other positive princess quite like YOU!

Q

Queen

Black girls with the right tools become black queens.

R

Respect

Black girl, you are worthy to both give & receive respect.

S

Studious

Black girl you are stoo-dee-us. You can learn anything you want!

T

Temple

Black girl you take care of yourself because you are a temple.

U

Unison

Black girls are at least twice as powerful in unison.

V

Vibrations

Black girl you are made of positive vibrations.

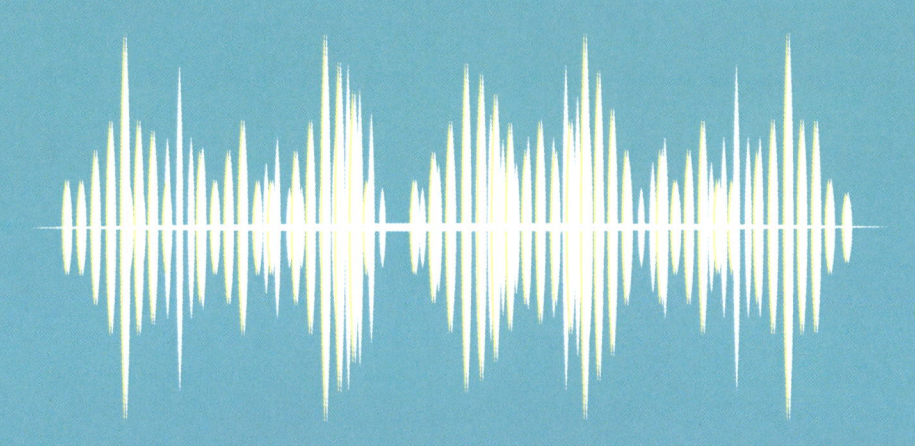

W

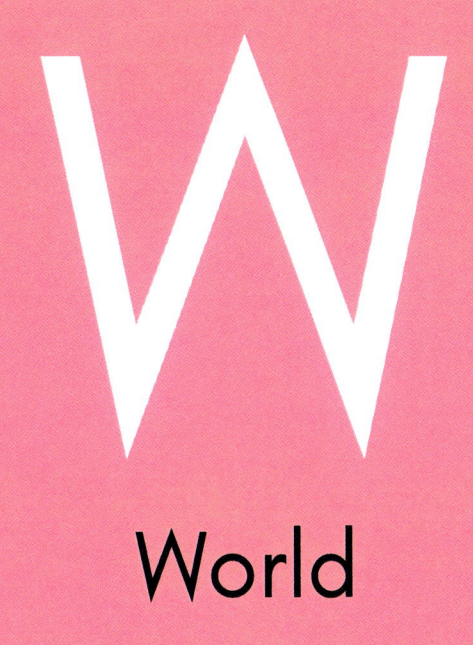

World

**Black girl you are a Light.
You matter in this world.**

X

Xylophone

Black girl, your personality is more colorful than a xylophone. That's what makes you interesting!

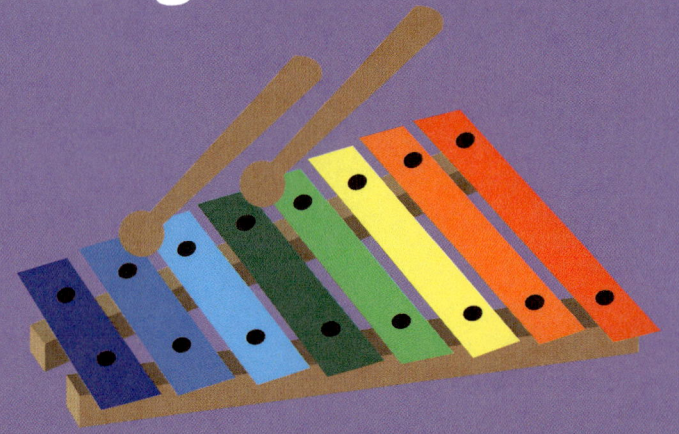

Y

Youth

Black girl, embrace your youth.

Z

Zero

Black girl, I counted how many mistakes God made on you and I came out to zero!

sun kissed
PUBLICATIONS, LLC

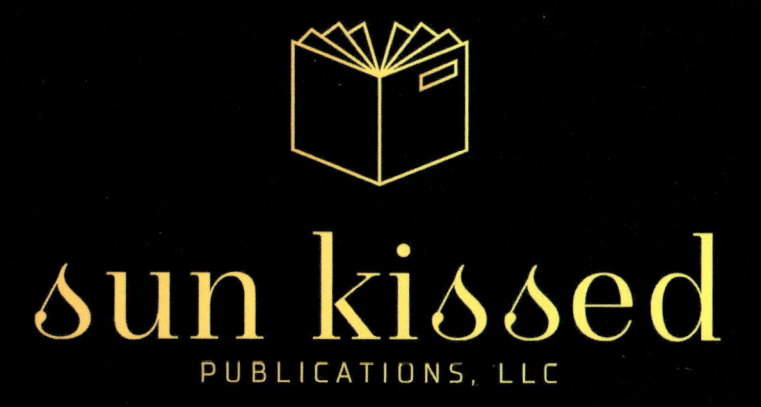

sunkissedpublications.org

© 2021 E'Nyah Reed

All rights reserved.